I Am Him
and
He Is Me

By

Jeffrey Horne

Illustrated by Taquon Middleton

To order additional copies of this book, contact:
Xlibris
844-714-8691
www.Xlibris.com
Orders@Xlibris.com

ISBN: Softcover   978-1-6698-2798-6
       EBook   978-1-6698-2797-9

Print information available on the last page

Rev. date: 06/08/2022

I would like to dedicate the book to my father Hubert S. Horne, my mother Maxine D. Horne and my brother Elias Horne for their loving support. To Ryqui, for your inspiration and for everything that you do for me and our son. Thank you all family and friends.

The book is also dedicated to the loving memory of:

Annie Clea Fox
Haywood T. Fox Jr.
Anthony D. Alexander Jr.

I am him and he is me, So he is

Caring

I am him and he is me. So you are

Compassionate

I am him and he is me. So you have a

Thirst for Knowledge

I am him and he is me. So you enjoy

Sharing

I am him and he is me. So you have a great

Sense of Humor

I am him and he is me. So you

Enjoy Life

I am him and he is me. So you are

Sensitive

I am him and he is me. So you understand the power of

Prayer

I am him and he is me.
So you know how to

Love

I am him and he is me.
So you are

Respectful

I am him and he is me. So you are

Courteous

I am him and he is me.
So you are a

Dreamer

Printed in the United States
by Baker & Taylor Publisher Services